WELCOME TO The Soulmate Scam

Falling in love with a narcissist sucks.
Help and hope is here!

An educational workbook for narcississtic abuse recovery.
Journaling prompts and coloring pages are included.

By: Katherine London, LCSW

Table of Contents

Welcome to the Soulmate Scam!

Has your dream relationship evolved into a nightmare? Are you wondering if your partner is a narcissist? Are you hoping the person you first met will resurface and things will get better again? If one or more of these questions are a yes, then this workbook is for you.

The term narcissist is thrown around a lot these days. And because narcissism is a spectrum, behavior can range from a bit self-absorbed to downright dangerous. As a therapist, I will tell you that many of the concepts which allow us to understand the narcissist aren't taught in graduate school and can't be found in clinical textbooks. Expressions such as crazymaking, gaslighting, flying monkeys, and crazymaking have evolved over time. They put meaning to the survivor's experience and help the healing process.

Narcissists are ironic in that they regard themselves as one of a kind special, yet all seem to use the same play book. *Welcome to the Shit Show* is the story of your romance with a narcissist from beginning to oh so predictable end. You will learn how you got here, the signs and symptoms of narcissism, as well as the types of emotional abuse that occur in these relationships. Tools for recovery are also included to help you become narc proof!

Things to keep in mind while using this workbook:

This content is intended for those who have had one or more romances with a narcissist and can be beneficial both during or after a relationship.

As narcissists are not exclusive to any gender, and gender is fluid, I will be using "they" when referring to the narcissist.

I often hear clients say "my narcissist" when speaking about a narcissistic partner. I prefer not to use that expression in these pages. Doing so acts as an emotional tie to that person. Let's start by making the shift in your head so that you can free them in real life to move on and far, far, away from you!

This workbook will support your healing journey. It does not take the place of professional help. Why? Because prolonged emotional abuse can lead to anxiety, depression, and PTSD, and these issues can require treatment.

You may feel certain you can diagnose your significant other as being on the spectrum of narcissism. Keep in mind that assessment by a qualified professional over time is needed to determine whether a person has personality issues. And at the end of the day, a partner who is toxic for you does not need a specific label to be recognized as such! Just take what you need and leave the rest.

As you navigate the recovery process remember that this is not a normal relationship or a normal breakup! And you didn't know what you didn't know. But you will now. And there is light at the end of the tunnel!

Love and virtual hugs,

Kathy

(Follow me on Instagram at @become_authentic_af)

SOULMATE SCAM

When you fall in love with a narcissist, sociopath or psychopath, it can feel at first as if you've met your soulmate. But as time passes and reality sets in, you will trade the happily ever after for an honorary degree in toxic relationships from the Universe's School of Hard Knocks. The good news? You will become one bad ass boss from this life experience. Narc proof baby.

What "soulmate" means to me...

_____
_____
_____
_____
_____

At first, my partner appeared to be my soulmate (describe)...

_____
_____
_____
_____
_____

But over time it became more like a soulmate scam because...

_____
_____
_____
_____
_____
_____
_____

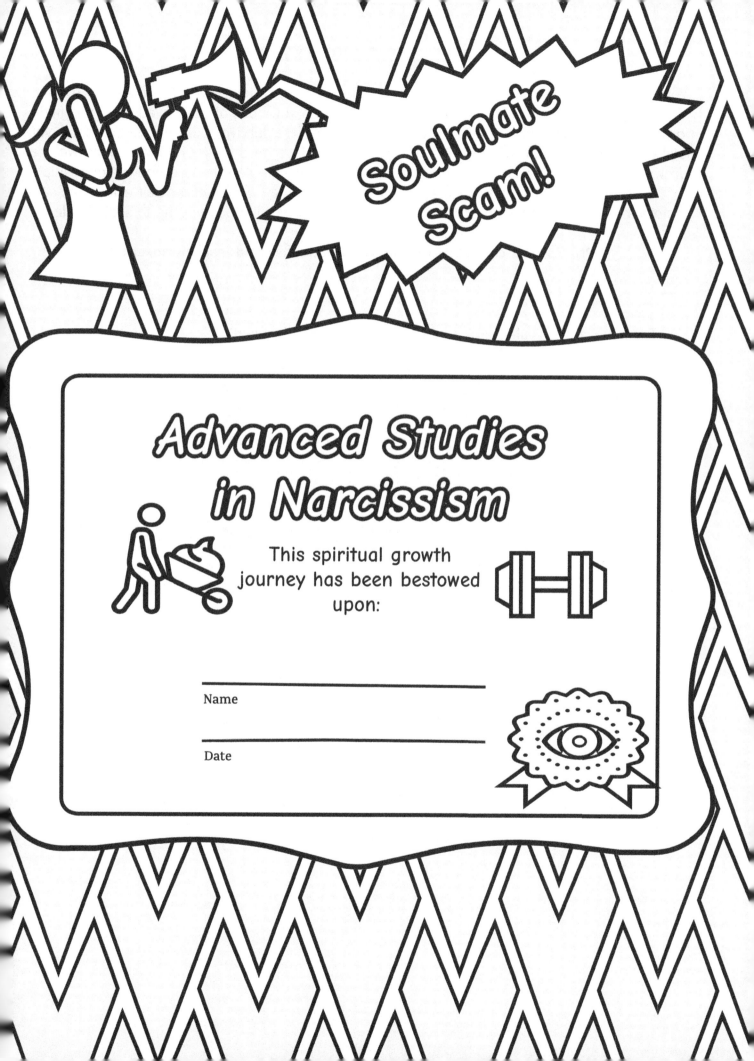

WHY? LIKE, SERIOUSLY, WHY?

Your past experiences make you vulnerable. Your kind spirit keeps you from leaving sooner. If your parent(s) or caregiver(s) are narcissistic, then you have already lived it, so this feels normal. Codependency and people pleasing behavior were survival skills in childhood. Do you still put others first and have trouble saying no? Don't be hard on yourself. As adults, we are drawn to the familiar, even if that is a shit show! Recently single after a crappy relationship? The narcissist will promise much better. Spoiler alert: they won't deliver. Self-esteem also factors in. Are you a quart low on self-love? The narcissist will build you up to seal the deal.

Pro tip: You can learn to retain that kindness and lose the takers.

I may have been vulnerable when I first met them (explain)...

_____

_____

_____

_____

On a 1-10 scale, I rate my self-esteem is a ___ but I'd like it to be a ___ (explain)...

_____

_____

_____

_____

Things I will work on now to reduce my vulnerability to a toxic partner include...

_____

_____

_____

_____

_____

_____

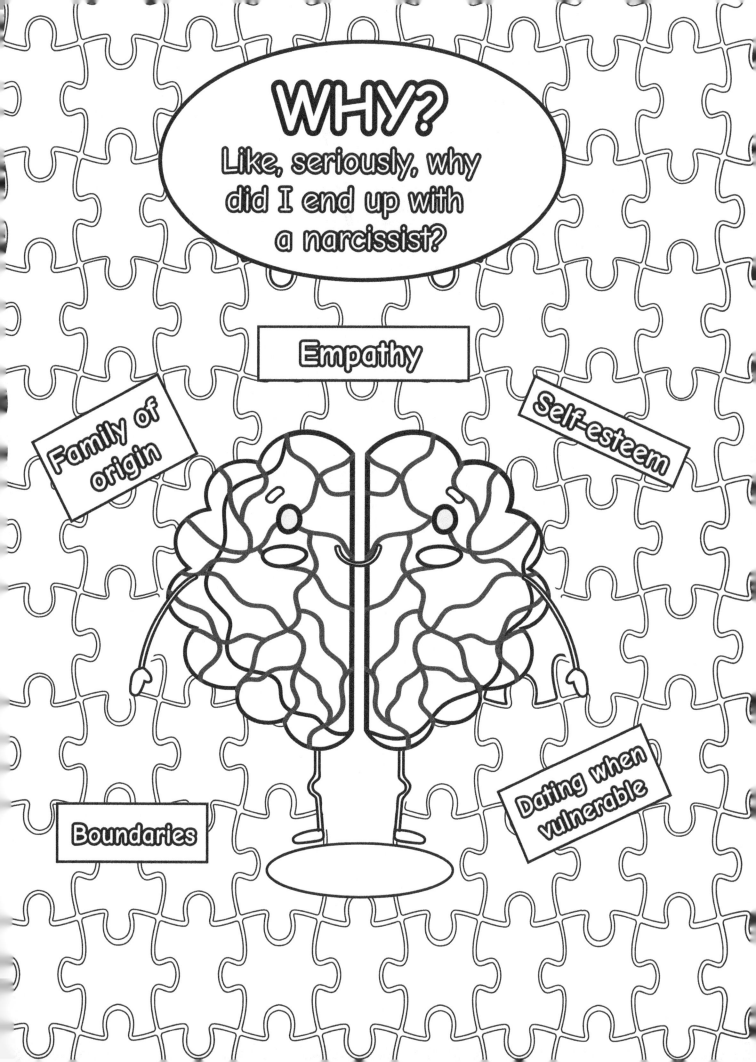

NARCISSIST

"Enough about me, let's talk about me!"
We will explore all things narcissist
in the coming pages. In short, they are
self-absorbed, lack empathy, feel entitled to do
whatever, whenever, and exploit others who don't
set good boundaries. This may present as super
self-assured or being the victim of multiple
dramas. They turn on the charm and tug at the
heart strings of the empath.

EMPATH

You've heard of being able to read the
room? Empaths kick it up a notch. They
are highly sensitive and drawn to helping
and healing others. Empaths can feel
another's pain. With such a big heart,
sometimes this can lead to giving too
much and being the target of toxic types
such as the narcissist.

My partner's behavior began to make me wonder when...

I think I am/am not an empath because...

I focused more on my partner's well-being than my own when...

YOU DIDN'T KNOW WHAT YOU DIDN'T KNOW

Wait, what? You didn't know your significant other was a narcissist? Maybe even a sociopath or a psychopath? Do you find yourself asking why, why, why, you didn't see the signs earlier? Umm, that's an easy one. Most kind people don't assume the worst about their partners. They give them the benefit of the doubt. When the person you love has been mirroring you (more about this toxic tactic later) it's easy to believe whatever they are selling. Healing begins with SELF-FORGIVENESS. So how about starting down that path right now instead of continuing to be your own worst critic? Because you didn't know what you didn't know.

Good news! Now. You. Do.

I can't believe I didn't see...

_____

_____

_____

_____

I even gave them the benefit of the doubt when (give examples)...

_____

_____

_____

_____

Check in: Working on self-forgiveness has been...

_____

_____

_____

_____

_____

THE FROG IN BOILING WATER

I'm not sure which one is more aggravating: When someone else asks why you stayed for so long in a toxic relationship or when you ask yourself the same question? The frog in boiling water story sums up this aspect of the shit show well. No frog would jump in a hot pot. Yet they would sit in a pot that's room temperature. When the heat goes up slowly, that froggy doesn't realize the water is boiling until it was too late. And yes, my love, in this story you are the frog.

Don't worry, there were no frogs harmed in the making of this analogy. Promise.

If I ask myself why I stayed (or am staying) for so long the answer is...

_____

_____

_____

_____

I relate to this frog's story because...

_____

_____

_____

_____

_____

I realized the "water was boiling" in our relationship when...

_____

_____

_____

_____

_____

_____

#1 EMPATHY

Wondering whether your true love has true nightmare potential? Look for the three E's. The first E is empathy (or lack thereof). Simply put, this E is in the low to no range. Narcissists lack the ability to appreciate what you're feeling and can't put themselves in your shoes emotionally. But they can fool you with cognitive empathy. This is when they recognize and respond according to social cues, for example, they see you cry and know they should offer support. Don't mistake this for feeling your pain! Think more along the lines of programmable artificial intelligence.

Pro tip: Don't expect the narcissist to apologize. Like ever. But stay long enough and they will find a way to blame YOU for their own bad behavior.

Ways to show empathy to a significant other include ....

_____

_____

_____

_____

I noticed they showed less empathy than I hoped for when...

_____

_____

_____

_____

My partner wasn't one to apologize or if they did it wasn't sincere because...

_____

_____

_____

_____

_____

#2 ENTITLEMENT

The 3 E's continue with entitlement or the belief that one deserves or has the right to something without any further explanation. Narcissists expect special treatment because they think they are better than others. Superior. The king (or queen) shit. This holier than though act is actually a cover for insecurity and low self-esteem. Narcissists expect to get what they want regardless of how they treat you and will take offense if you respond to their request with a "no". When you do supply them with whatever they desire, don't expect a thank you, any personal loans to be repaid, or promises to be kept.

My partner acted in an entitled manner when ...

_____

_____

_____

_____

When I said no, it would lead to the following reactions (examples)...

_____

_____

_____

_____

They did/didn't apologize for_____which made me feel...

_____

_____

_____

_____

_____

Entitlement

Automatic Compliance

Their way or you will pay. Their interests come first.

Special Privileges

They treat themselves to only the best!

A Free Pass For All Bad Behavior

But don't expect an apology!

Your Resources

Your money is their money. Your casa is their casa.

Credit For Everything

Even when you did it.

Your Back Up Resources

That rainy day fund, your home's equity, the retirement account...

#3 EXPLOITATION

Give and take is normal in a healthy relationship. Take and take (and take) better explains the narcissistic approach to a relationship. Narcissists target kind people with loose boundaries. And by this I mean trouble saying no, not loose as in slutty. They will manipulate your emotions to get their way even when doing so is harmful to your well being. Over time, your money, your resources, and your sanity slowly slip away as you wait for the "help" you've been giving them to be reciprocated or to improve the relationship. Exploitation completes the 3 E's.

I started to feel taken advantage of when...

_____

_____

_____

_____

I wanted to say no to certain things, but I didn't because...

_____

_____

_____

_____

I thought giving so much_____in my relationship would _____ but instead it...

_____

_____

_____

_____

_____

_____

EXPLOITATION

NARCISSISM IS A SPECTRUM

Narcissism isn't a yes or no type of situation. It ranges from annoying to unrelenting to dangerous. Assessment over time by a qualified professional is needed. On the low end of the spectrum is someone with narcissistic tendencies or traits. This is when your boo is a bit too self-absorbed. In the middle, we have a diagnosis of narcissistic personality disorder, which involves a fixed set of maladaptive thoughts and behaviors. NPD persists throughout life and make long term relationships hard to maintain (Read: Just about impossible.)
At the high end of the spectrum is malignant narcissism. This person has symptoms of anti-social personality disorder. APD doesn't equate to being a loner, it's more a lack of respect for social norms, the law, or even your life.

Bottom line: Toxic is toxic. Your sanity and safety are more important than any label!

I view them as mild/medium/super-duper toxic on the narcissism spectrum because...

_____

_____

_____

Their past relationship patterns show me_____about who they really are...

_____

_____

_____

_____

I do/don't see this person as capable of change (explain)...

_____

_____

_____

_____

_____

OVERT VS. COVERT?

I used to think all narcissists were obvious. You've seen them. Flashy, confident, always bragging about their accomplishments? This is the case for the classic or "overt" narcissist. They are grandiose, enjoy the spotlight, and seek your never ending admiration. However, sometimes the devil doesn't show up with pointy horns and a red cape. Sometimes they present as everything you ever wanted! Enter the vulnerable or "covert" narcissist. A real life wolf in sheep's clothing. Initially, this type is hard to spot. They may seem humble, self-effacing, and sensitive. A wounded soul. This is just another persona used to suck you in.

The reality: At the end of the day, you're looking at two sides of the same coin. RUN.

I think my partner was overt/covert (explain)...

.I can/can't relate to being with a wolf in sheep's clothing...

Things I didn't realize about narcissism until now include...

Overt vs. Covert Narcissists

RELATIONSHIP STAGES WITH A NARCISSIST

News flash! You don't need a crystal ball to predict the progression of a romantic relationship with a narcissist. While they may fancy themselves as one of a kind, the reality is narcissists all use the same playbook. So as sure as bubble gum will stick to the bottom of your shoe, a narcissist will cycle through these three stages. You will be idealized, devalued, and then discarded. Stay with the same narcissist long enough and you can repeat these three phases over and over. FOR YEARS.

Icky truth: During the discard, the narcissist is already lining up someone new to idealize.

My partner made me feel special in the beginning by (examples)...

_____

_____

_____

_____

_____

Being idealized didn't last and I began to feel devalued when...

_____

_____

_____

_____

_____

The discard happened when...

_____

_____

_____

_____

_____

DROP THE MASK

Narcissists show you whom they think you want to see to get what they want. They wear a "mask". This fake version of themselves could make them seem important, capable, charming, helpful, patient, kind, and sensitive. They will align with what appeals to you. But over time, the narcissist's actions and patterns tell you who they really are. Raging and self-centered with low or no empathy. They fake and they take. Until you wake.

Keeping it real: When you begin to question what's beneath the mask, threats of a discard aren't far behind.

When we first met it seemed like we had so much in common (list)...

_____

_____

_____

_____

Ways I saw their "mask" slip (discuss)...

_____

_____

_____

_____

As the relationship progressed, I saw my partner's personality change...

_____

_____

_____

_____

_____

_____

NARCISSISTIC SUPPLY

A car needs fuel to run. A vampire is fueled by blood. Okay, I don't know if vampires are really a thing, but it sure makes for a great analogy about your relationship with a narcissist! The narcissist needs their own kind of fuel, which is called "supply". And baby that's YOU. They scope out partners that can offer whatever is needed to reinforce whatever keeps them feeling good about themselves. This could be your unending adoration, money, sex...the list is endless. They target nice people who suck at saying no and deplete you of your resources. When it's evident that you have nothing left to give, they will line up new supply and discard you.

Fun fact: Even when everything seems great between the narcissist and their new boo, it's not. That person is supply too. And so it goes.

I gave my partner their "supply" through (money, attention, sex, etc.)...

_____

_____

_____

_____

I began to feel drained by their demands (give examples)...

_____

_____

_____

If I'm honest with myself, the relationship started to go downhill when...

_____

_____

_____

_____

_____

Narcissistic Supply
(Fuel for the Narcissist)

They target those who are kind and have trouble setting limits

When the supply is used up, the narcissist moves on to a new source.

MIRRORING

When a narcissist has their eyes on you romantically speaking, they will literally have their eyes on you. This involves observing your non-verbal behavior and mirroring it - from mannerisms, and movements to changes in posture. They will also emotionally mirror you by appearing to have the same issues, thoughts, and feelings about life. Humans are hard wired to feel attracted to those who are similar and mirroring serves to disarm a person so they feel more comfortable, relaxed, and understood. Who doesn't want that? Before you think you've hit all six numbers in the lotto of love, STOP. The truth is mirroring is a tactic used to lock in the narcissistic supply.

Educated buyer beware: It's also a sales strategy. People who want your business have done this forever. And who is a narcissist if not a great salesperson?

Ways I was being mirrored non-verbally (describe)...

_____

_____

_____

_____

They also mirrored my beliefs by saying...

_____

_____

_____

_____

When someone likes everything I like it makes me feel...

_____

_____

_____

_____

_____

IDEALIZE

This new relationship seems AMAZING. (Cue the heart eyes). You're sure you've met the one! But if that one is a narcissist, then this isn't a true soulmate experience. It's a soulmate scam. You are being idealized. Put on a pedestal and showered with praise, promises, affection, and attention. Things move fast and feel intense. The narcissist is on their best behavior while you are treated like the queen/king you've always wanted to be! Why? Because the narcissist sees you as a reflection of themselves. If you are perfect in their eyes, it is even more proof to the world of how superior they are. The length of time for this stage varies. But it is NEVER forever.

Next up: Love bombing.

In the beginning, they complimented me by...

And I felt so special when...

In retrospect, the attention was too much too soon because...

IDEALIZE

LOVE BOMBING

Love bombing is a tool used by the narcissist while you are being idealized. The narcissist flatters you, gives gifts, and professes their everlasting love waaaaay too soon in order to speed up the relationship. How is love bombing different than falling in love the healthier way?
It's simple. Unions grow based on shared experiences and trust over time.
You can't rush the real stuff. Love bombing is mistaking intensity for intimacy.

Ways that I have been love bombed (list)....

My partner came on strong too soon by doing the following...

I felt they were trying to speed up the relationship when...

"THE CRAZY EX"

You can count on death and taxes. You can also count on the narcissist informing you that their ex or exes are crazy. Bipolar is also a popular term used incorrectly by the narcissist to describe their previous "soulmate". What they fail to mention is that it was the narcissist who drove that person to the brink of insanity. Don't get me wrong, there are bona fide crazy exes out there and having one doesn't make someone a narcissist. But let this revelation be an opportunity to do some further investigation. Is there a long list of crazy exes? Does your boo blame all of their problems on these exes? Or did they learn something about themselves in the process and take responsibility for their part?

Moving forward: Listen carefully as you get to know someone. There are clues to be heard from DAY ONE.

My partner told me the following bad things about the exes...

_____

_____

_____

_____

Ways they didn't take accountability for their previous relationships...

_____

_____

_____

_____

In the future I will respond to someone talking about their crazy ex by...

_____

_____

_____

_____

_____

The "Crazy" Ex

Cra-zy (Adjective)

Someone who has been emotionally abused, financially depleted, lied to, and cheated on by the narcissist. (Synonyms: bipolar, bitch.)

THE DANGLING CARROT

At the beginning a relationship with a narcissist, you will be promised the moon. Or maybe I should say the sun because these promises will make everything about your future together look so bright! Dangled in front of you, just out of your grasp, you won't question the failure of these promises to come through for quite some time. And when you do, count on a compelling excuse to keep you hanging on a little longer. Or you may be the lucky recipient of a guilt trip that makes you apologize for even asking!

The cliff notes: Also known as FUTURE FAKING, the dangling carrot will leave you high, dry, and realizing it was all a lie.

At the beginning of the relationship, I thought our future together would be...

Some of the promises that were made to me included...

They did/didn't keep their word when (give examples)...

DEVALUE

When you first meet the narcissist, you are treated so well that you think you've found your soulmate. But over time the idealizing stops and devaluing takes its place. Examples of being devalued include put downs which are subtle at first, withdrawal of affection, raging at you or the silent treatment. You see, the narcissist is not capable of keeping up the charade that hooked you. And when you notice these behavior changes you will want to talk about it. While requesting to discuss problems would be A-okay in a healthy relationship, a narcissist will instead make excuses or blame you. Being devalued serves the purpose of taking the focus off the narcissist's behavior so you start to question yourself instead of them.

Truth bomb: Sorry sis (or bro) but as your mental confusion becomes the norm, mind games played by the narcissist do too.

I felt devalued when...

At first, I thought this change in their behavior was due to...

I coped with their treatment of me by...

Devalue

CRAZYMAKING

Is it a word in the dictionary? No. Does it describe what it's like to be in a relationship with a narcissist? Yes, yes, and furthermore yes. Crazymaking is a catch all term for all the tactics used by the narcissist that make you feel off balance, frustrated, exasperated, and ready to pull your hair out. Raise your hand, or just roll your eyes in disgust, if any of these examples ring a bell: Did they try to convince you that the awful thing they did never happened? Or try to blame you instead? Do they behave hypocritically (telling you to go easy on the spending while they treat themselves)? When you attempt to resolve the conflict, expect a dose of explosive rage and/or silent treatment. This is punishment for you having the nerve to question their bad behavior.

Spoiler alert: It's not you, but give them enough time and you'll start to believe it is.

Things about this relationship that made me feel crazy (give examples)...

_____

_____

_____

_____

There were even times when no matter what I did it was wrong (explain)...

_____

_____

_____

_____

But when I pointed out the actual problem, they would...

_____

_____

_____

_____

_____

GASLIGHTING

Gaslighting is a form of emotional abuse that the narcissist uses to avoid responsibility for their behavior. They lie, deny, and even project the blame onto you, the victim, who is then left confused and filled with self doubt. It is crazymaking! Imagine the narcissist with their hand still in the cookie jar, crumbs on their face, and it's YOU that gets yelled at for eating all the cookies.

Truth be told: It's all a shell game.

I now know I was being gaslighted when...

_____

_____

_____

_____

_____

They would deny the truth even when I could prove it (give examples)...

_____

_____

_____

_____

There were times when was told something was my fault when it wasn't...

_____

_____

_____

_____

_____

_____

NARCISSISTIC INJURY

Peekaboo! I see you! Such a fun game to play with a baby. But not so enjoyable to engage in with an adult who is acting like a baby. In short, a narcissistic injury can be caused by any perceived rejection such as you saying no, maintaining a boundary, and the uber insult - going no contact. The narcissist tries to control you by presenting a fake shell of a person (the mask) which is used to cover up the insecure, fragile mess inside. Your compliance is necessary to keep up the charade and now you aren't playing by the rules.

I say: Good for you. It's about time.

When I say/said no to my partner....

_____

_____

_____

_____

Setting limits/boundaries with my partner went something like this...

_____

_____

_____

_____

_____

I decided to go no contact because_____or if I'm thinking about it due to...

_____

_____

_____

_____

_____

NARCISSISTIC RAGE

Are you familiar with the concept of emotional intelligence (EQ)? It involves the awareness of and ability to cope with emotions in a healthy grown up kind of way. Well, narcissistic rage sure as shit isn't that! Do *not* expect a narcissist to sit down and calmly reflect on what they are feeling. Do *not* expect them to empathize with what you are feeling and collaborate with you to resolve conflict. Narcissistic rage is a response to a narcissistic injury (you hurt their little baby feelings). It is an extreme reaction to what is typically an average situation and can show up as prolonged silent treatment or explosive anger. Or both.

Truth by told: It's the go to coping skill for all things that don't go their way.

I think healthy ways to handle conflict in a relationship include...

My partner dealt with our disagreements by...

Examples of times they really overreacted...

THE SILENT TREATMENT

What does a little kid do when they don't get their way? The have an explosion. Or an implosion. When the narcissist doesn't pitch a fit (narcissistic rage), then they may pitch a pout - also known as the silent treatment. This tactic serves to manipulate and control you. It shows ZERO regard for your feelings and is emotionally abusive. Period.

Do: Expect more anxiety and less self-esteem when this happens to you repeatedly.
Don't: Expect to understand why they behaved this way in the first place.

The silent treatment happened if...

When my partner did not/does not speak to me (discuss your feelings)...

In order to cope with the silent treatment I would...

TRAUMA BONDING

A relationship with a narcissist is like riding a roller coaster. The highs seem amazing and come with a burst of feel good brain chemistry. Then the bottom drops out and brings lows that are downright depressing. In a healthy relationship, you bond with your partner through trust and intimacy. Slow and steady wins the race. The bond with a narcissist starts with love bombing and once you're hooked, the emotional roller coaster begins. Alternating between hurtful head games and over the top attention becomes the norm. You are addicted to the highs and devastated by the lows. That's why the discard feels like the worst pain in the world. *You're detoxing.*

Get off this ride. It is nothing more than a house of mirrors.

When things were good they were really good (describe)...

_____

_____

_____

There were other times I was treated so badly (list some)...

_____

_____

_____

The thought of being without my partner is/was (explain)...

_____

_____

_____

_____

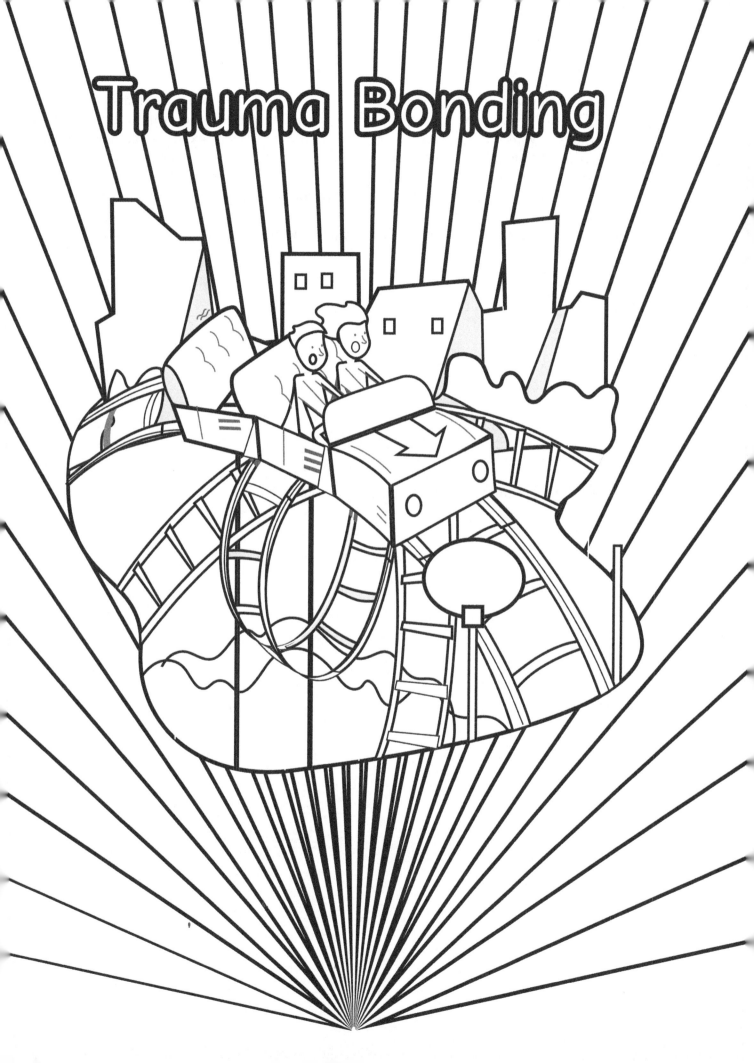

FOG: FEAR, OBLIGATION & GUILT

Why does someone stay in a toxic relationship? Much like the picture to the right, it's complicated. Let's simplify. The F.O.G. acronym is a good place to start. These are three of the most common reasons for remaining with a narcissist. It also refers to the brain "fog" experienced when you are up to your eyeballs in emotional abuse as self-doubt goes up while self-esteem goes down. Other reasons for not leaving include embarrassment, shame, financial stress, religious beliefs, and normalizing the abuse due to your own previous experiences with similar personalities.

Post relationship promise: The F.O.G. will clear and the sun will come out again.

When I think about this relationship ending I fear(ed)...

_____

_____

_____

_____

I thought I was obligated to stay with them because...

_____

_____

_____

_____

The idea of the relationship being over makes/made me feel guilty due to...

_____

_____

_____

_____

_____

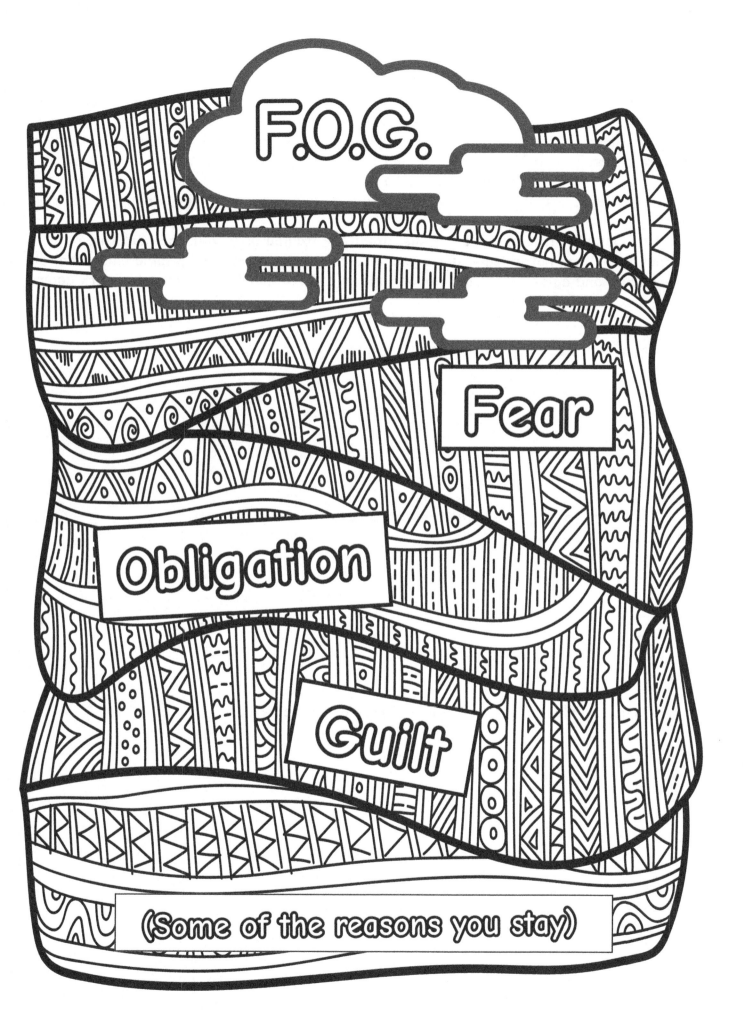

THE DISCARD

After being devalued and devalued and devalued, the discard becomes the last phase of the relationship with a narcissist. It can happen for two reasons: 1. You are no longer a good source of narcissistic supply (this is code for they've depleted you and they've found someone else with more resources) OR 2. You've finally set some limits with them because you are seeing through their crap. In the latter situation, the narcissist experiences a narcissistic injury due to fear of rejection which often leads to them breaking up with you first so they can feel in control.

Truth bomb: When you are being discarded, the trauma bond with the narcissist flare. You may BEG them not to leave, apologize for something, or even many somethings, that aren't your fault, and agree to violate your own moral code to make the relationship work again.

The end of our relationship was prompted by myself/my partner...

_____

_____

_____

In an attempt to prevent the breakup, I did the following....

_____

_____

_____

_____

I had trouble accepting the end of the relationship because...

_____

_____

_____

_____

Baby, it's cold outside

The Discard

NO CLOSURE

SPOILER ALERT: There will be NO closure with a narcissist. Nada. Nothing. Zilch. Why? Because they have moved on without regard to your feelings. You are no longer a good source of "supply" and they have no use for you. They don't think of you as a person who is in need of an explanation. And attempting to get closure will only result in more gaslighting and victim blaming. The REAL closure happens when you see this soul mate scammer as a life lesson. A master class on narcissistic abuse.

DO NOT DESPAIR: Want to be narc proof? Helpful tips and tools are coming up.

Closure after a relationship happens by....

Ways I attempted to get closure...

The following issues were left unresolved...

THE MONSTER YOU SEE AT THE END

Questions you may ask yourself when the relationship with
a narcissist is circling the drain or has ended:

Perhaps they are under a lot of stress and this is just a rough patch?
Maybe they don't realize how hurtful their words and actions are?
Perhaps with love and patience they will become their old self again?
What if all those "crazy exes" have made them jaded and I
can make them see I am different?

**Answer: No, no, and furthermore no. You learn a lot more about a person at
the end of the relationship than at the start of one.**

Things that really shocked me about their behavior during/after the breakup...

_____

_____

_____

Even so, I made the following excuses for them...

_____

_____

_____

Those actions taught me...

_____

_____

_____

_____

SMEAR CAMPAIGN

And even when it's over, it's not always over. Remember that narcissism is a spectrum and when they are high in toxic behaviors it can get worse before it gets better. This is because when a narcissist can no longer control you, they will try to control what other people think about you. Consider a smear campaign the grand finale of your relationship with a narcissist. This can range from spreading rumors around town to attacks on your personal and professional reputation. Can you say vindictive? Smear campaigns can take a huge toll on your sanity, so seek out personal and professional support when needed.

**Remember: Sometimes lies take the elevator and truth takes the stairs.
Hang in there.**

When someone spreads lies about me it feels....

I found out they were telling other people things such as_____about me...

I think the worst part of being smeared is/would be...

Smear Campaign

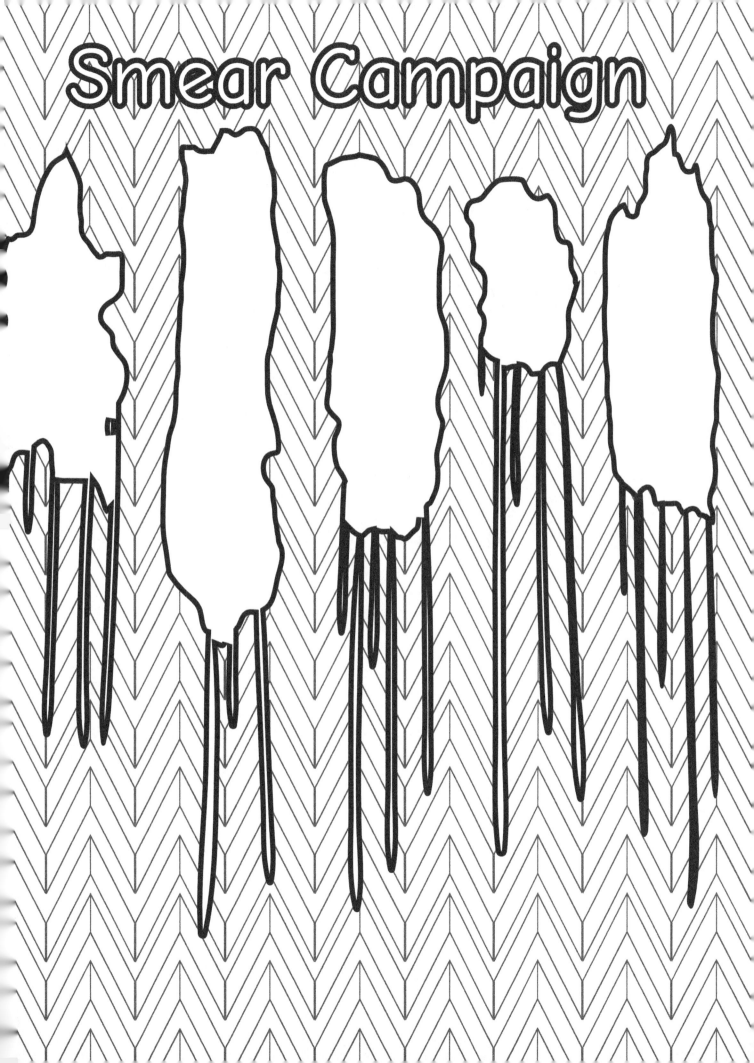

FLYING MONKEYS

Ahh, if it isn't the flying monkeys. Remember the cackling little creatures who surrounded the Wicked Witch of the West? For those of you who were born after Gen X, I'm talking about the Wizard of Oz. In this case, the term flying monkeys describes people that the narcissist recruits to behave negatively towards you. They believe what the toxic person has told them as fact. Think narcissistic abuse by proxy. (Also known as third grade on the playground bullshit.) A flying monkey might be a family member (theirs or yours), coworker, mutual friend, or even a member of your church.

FUN FACT: As you recover from narcissistic abuse you may see that YOU TOO were once made into a flying monkey by the narcissist. You remember, back when you thought they were telling the truth about those "crazy" exes? Forgive yourself. Hindsight is 20/20.

Some people I knew who took their side and became flying monkeys did so by...

_____

_____

_____

Negative treatment that I experienced from others due to my partner included...

_____

_____

_____

At the start of our relationship, they tried to (or did) make me a flying monkey by...

_____

_____

_____

NO CONTACT RULE

The no contact rule is the most effective method (when possible) for recovering from narcissistic abuse. I say when possible because you may share a child with the narcissist in which case the gray rock method is a more realistic strategy. No contact can be difficult - like coming off an addictive substance. Especially when the narcissist circles back (a.k.a. "hoovers") and tries to convince you this roller coaster relationship is worth another shot!

PRO TIP: Expect a meltdown of toddler like proportions when you first cut off contact. Like any fire, without oxygen, it will eventually extinguish itself. Stay firm. It's worth it.

The idea of going no contact makes me feel...

_____

_____

_____

_____

Even when I tried to do this, I still kept tabs on them by...

_____

_____

_____

_____

_____

My ex responded to my choosing to go no contact by... (Or I think they would...)

_____

_____

_____

_____

_____

GRAY ROCK METHOD

When you can't go no contact, the gray rock method is another tool to distance yourself from the toxic person. The end goal is to get off their radar.. You throw fuel on the fire by reacting, explaining, taking offense, and showing emotion. Narcissists get energy (supply) from this! Remember, negative attention is better than no attention. Instead, aim to extinguish the flames by appearing uninteresting. You are a gray rock. Unaffected.

I use gray rock rather than no contact because...

_____

_____

_____

_____

As I first started gray rocking, the following happened...

_____

_____

_____

_____

As I practice gray rock, I am careful not to take the bait when...

_____

_____

_____

_____

_____

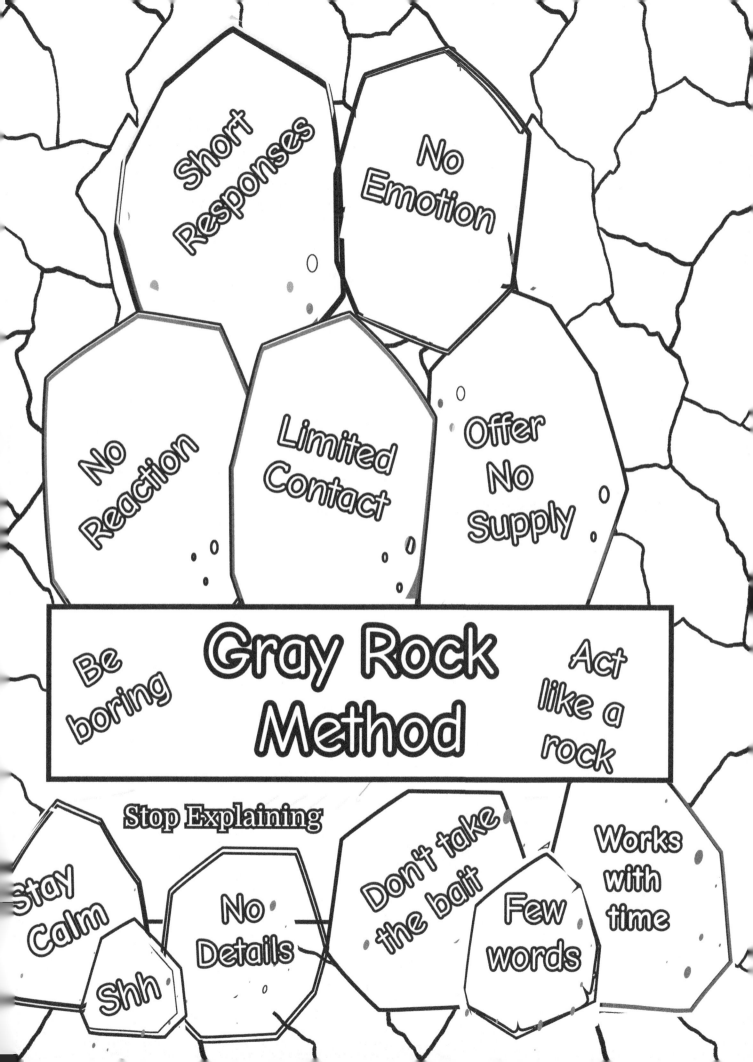

OBSERVE. DON'T ABSORB.

Being in the presence of a narcissist can be EXHAUSTING. Why? Because you are sensitive, caring, and take their words to heart. Better boundaries are the way out of this vicious cycle when you can't go no contact. The gray rock method takes time. It involves learning not to take the bait. This stops providing the narcissist with the reaction they are so desperately seeking. Instead, imagine you are coated with the same stuff they put on non-stick cookware. Listen and then let it slide right off. You are granite, baby. Impenetrable.

When I am around someone who pushes my buttons, I feel...

_____

_____

_____

_____

_____

When I do "take the bait" it prolongs the argument because...

_____

_____

_____

_____

_____

I can visualize myself observing not absorbing (describe)...

_____

_____

_____

_____

_____

_____

Observe.
Don't absorb.

RESPOND DON'T REACT

We've talked about narcissistic supply (that's you boo). And that this supply is the fuel that keeps the narcissist energized. Negative attention works just as well to fill their tank. Therefore, when you don't engage, they will try repeatedly to provoke you. You will be tempted to argue back by offering lengthy explanations to get them to see the error of their ways. Break the pattern by going no contact or practicing gray rock. Observe, don't absorb. And respond don't react.

Tips of the trade: DO expect pushback when you start using these tools. It means they are working! Narcissists are you used to playing by the rules - their rules.
DON'T, I repeat DO NOT, react when baited. It makes you like a hamster in a wheel.
Running and running but not going anywhere.

The benefits of trying this technique for me would be...

Examples of how I can respond instead of react include...

I will be prepared for the following behavior from them when I do this...

THE FROG AND THE SCORPION

Did you ever hear the story about the frog and the scorpion? The tale of these two creatures explains the narcissist and empath dynamic well. One day, the scorpion, who could not swim, asked the frog for a ride across the river. The nice frog said yes, making only one request. "Just don't sting me! It will be the end for the both of us!" The scorpion agreed and they set out across the river. Alas, before they both made it to the other side, the scorpion did sting the frog. "But why?" asked the frog as they both began to sink below the surface. "Because it's my nature," said the scorpion.

Keeping it real: No matter how hard you try, a relationship with a narcissist is doomed from day one. They don't change. But the good news is you can!

This story made me think/feel......

_____

_____

_____

_____

When I met them, I thought they shared my morals and values (give examples).

_____

_____

_____

_____

I can see now that we do not share similar values because...

_____

_____

_____

_____

The Frog & The Scorpion

HOOVERING

Narcissists often return to the scene of the crime and try and rekindle the relationship. (a.k.a. the "hoover."). Think *Hoover* as in the vacuum cleaner because they are trying to suck you back into their web. How do they do it? They may claim to have seen the light and can't live without you! Throw in some more love bombing for good measure. Or, if your price of admission is lower than that, they may just say they missed you. Take them back and DO expect the following: Wash, rinse, repeat. I mean idealize, devalue, discard.

Bottom line: Nothing. Has. Changed.

I have/have not experienced hoovering (explain)...

_____

_____

_____

_____

I think my ex is/isn't capable of change because...

_____

_____

_____

_____

If my ex hoovered back into my life, I would...

_____

_____

_____

_____

_____

THIS IS NOT A NORMAL BREAKUP!

When the romantic relationship ends with a narcissist, it takes more than a band aid and a pint of Ben & Jerry's to recover. The narcissist leaves you with more questions than answers. It's hard to try and make peace with the lack of closure while recovering from the effects of prolonged emotional abuse. But why stop there? After this breakup you can be the subject of lies, half-truths, and attacks on your reputation. Depending on where the narcissist is in the spectrum of toxicity, your safety could even be at risk.

Ironic but true: The same person who made you feel safe enough to share all of your vulnerabilities at the start of the relationship will now use that information against you without so much as batting an eyelash. Nothing is off limits.

This breakup was different for me because...

_____

_____

_____

_____

The hardest part has been...

_____

_____

_____

_____

After our breakup there were things that made it harder to move on such as ...

_____

_____

_____

_____

_____

This is NOT a Normal Breakup

Turn your wounds
into wisdom,
and remember
healing takes time.

H.O.P.E. (Hold On Pain Ends)

Breakups suck. And we've established this is NOT a normal breakup. You are still putting the pieces of this soulmate scam together. Grief comes in waves. You will mourn the loss of the future you thought you had and the loss of innocence you'll never get back. So ride those waves. The pain WILL end. The key to healing is education, support, and a lots of self-love.

Hold on. Pain ends. That day is coming. And you will be so much better off for it.

I have been coping with this breakup by...

The pain from this relationship (feels/felt) like...

I will know I am getting better when...

(Hold On Pain Ends)

RELATIONSHIP RED FLAGS

It's time for some Monday morning quarter backing. Take a deep dive into your past relationship(s) and look for the red flags that you may have missed. This can prevent another shit show! Consider the beginning of each relationship like an interview process. You are learning things about your potential partner both by what they say and the actions they take. A red flag is not always a deal breaker, but it is a signal to PAUSE and look at the bigger picture. Monitor these actions and look for patterns over time. Do you relate to any of the red flag examples on the following page?

If a red flag is detected. STOP. Breathe in and out. Otherwise you'll get dizzy. Above all, remember to TRUST YOUR GUT.

The first time I remember noticing a red flag, I dealt with it by...

Looking back there were more of them than I realized, such as...

I will deal with red flags in the future by...

BOUNDARIES

Hey, you left the gate open. By this I mean your metaphorical gate. Narcissists look for partners who have difficulty setting and sticking to their limits (boundaries). We all have likes and dislikes as well as deal breakers. If you are a people pleaser it's easy to get overly invested in your partner's happiness at the expense of your own. Boundaries can be emotional, spiritual, physical, financial...you name it! They are to be respected by significant others. Give some thought to your boundaries and start sticking to them. This means saying no when needed, and even modifying the relationship when a boundary is ignored.

Here's some homework: Take note of how a person reacts when you say no.
Do you get the silent treatment? A full on hissy fit? Narcissists DO NOT like the word no.
Of course only YOU know your situation. So, safety first.

I think I do/don't need to work on my boundaries (explain)....

_____

_____

_____

My partner didn't respect my boundaries when...

_____

_____

_____

From now on I will respond to these situations by...

_____

_____

_____

_____

Boundaries

EDUCATED EMPATH

Do you want to keep the mosquitoes away? Get some bug repellent. Do you want to keep the human equivalent of mosquitoes away and never get caught up in this shit show again? Educate yourself about narcissism. And sociopathy/psychopathy. Then all the flavors in between. Work on healthier boundaries. That way when you recognize the red flags they can be addressed rather than swept under the carpet. The universe may not prevent you from meeting another narcissist (they walk among us), but self-awareness and an improved ability to stand up for yourself is a game changer.

My partner exploited my kindness by...

_____

_____

_____

_____

Ways I am practicing being an educated empath are...

_____

_____

_____

_____

As an educated empath I can protect myself from...

_____

_____

_____

_____

PSSST...

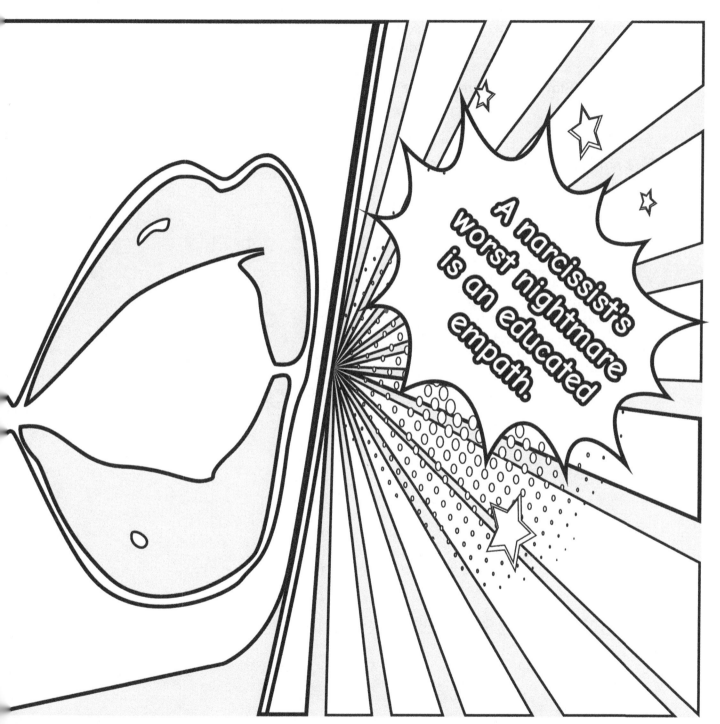

A narcissist's worst nightmare is an educated empath.

Educated empath: Puts self love first, spots and addressess any red flags, practices healthy boundaries, and understands the spectrum of narcissism. Chooses to opt out of toxic relationships.

TOXIC PEOPLE

Consider this a bonus page as you look beyond the romantic relationship to all of the people who are important in your life. Family, friends, coworkers, etc. You are starting to practice the skills needed to be the new improved 2.0 version of yourself. And this is something for your significant others to celebrate, support, and encourage. Right? Well, that depends. When you become more assertive, you may get some attitude. From whom? The same people that are used to taking advantage of you.

Stay woke friend: You've come too far to only come this far.

I've noticed there are other unhealthy relationships in my life as well...

I have dealt with these people (family, friends coworkers) in the following ways...

I think now I will also do the following...

Bad Ass Boss Award

You are a bad ass boss. Did you know that? Well then own it! Surviving narcissistic abuse takes incredible strength. You are awakening to the reality that the monster wasn't under the bed. They were **IN** your bed. As a result of this experience, you will emerge stronger and wiser. You are progressing in the journey towards your best self.

The end goal: Loving a narcissist is a life altering experience and leaves you with a kind of wisdom that not everyone has. Use it don't lose it.

I really need to give myself more credit for.....

_____

_____

_____

_____

_____

I feel wiser than I once was when it comes to.....

_____

_____

_____

_____

_____

I will use the following positive affirmations:

_____

_____

_____

_____

_____

SELF CARE LOOKS GOOD ON YOU!

As the dust settles, you will continue to gain new insights into your past relationship(s) and use this knowledge to take better care of the most important person of all. You! These life lessons have added tools to the emotional toolbox. Therapy with a counselor who understands narcissism and emotional abuse will also help with this process. If you are someone that tends to put others first, shift the focust to learning what makes YOU tick. What is needed to be your best self emotionally and physically? It's time to expect more from significant others than you once did and make a practice of not settling for less.

Guess what? Trusting your gut, addressing the elephant in the room, and saying things like no, hell no, or not today Satan will get easier. You're going to like this new you. Self-love first. NARC PROOF.

I have realized the following about my past romantic relationship(s)...

_____

_____

_____

_____

I am taking care of myself in the following ways...

_____

_____

_____

_____

I will do the following things if I sense a potential partner is toxic for me...

_____

_____

_____

_____

Self-Care Looks Good on you!

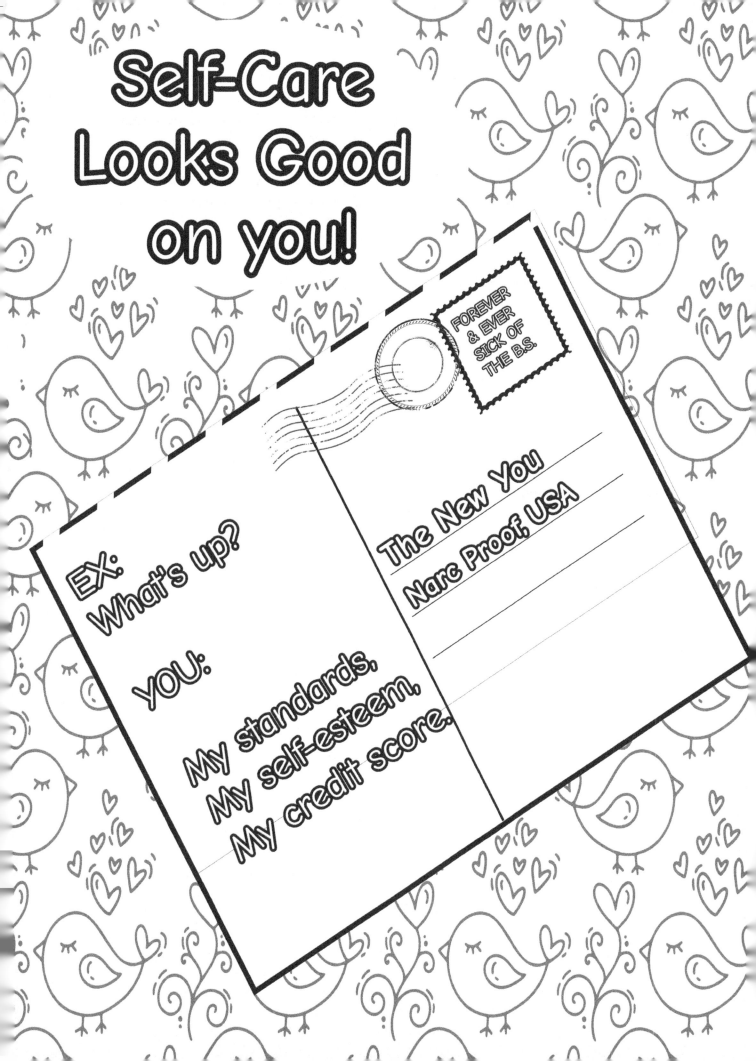

FOREVER & EVER SICK OF THE B.S.

EX:
What's up?

YOU:

My standards,
My self-esteem,
My credit score.

The New You
Narc Proof, USA

WOKE A.F.

I'm talking about your spiritual awakening. What? You said you're already in touch with your higher power? Well, my dear, congratulations! You have reached the next level in your spiritual growth journey. As a result of this experience, you'll approach all your relationships with a new set of eyes. And you may even realize this isn't your first rodeo with a narcissist.

Good news: Now you can see them coming. You will start to sense the energies of others (both dark and light) and learn to protect yours.

I have learned some life lessons from this experience such as...

_____

_____

_____

_____

I will no longer tolerate...

_____

_____

_____

_____

I am a better version of myself now because...

_____

_____

_____

_____

_____

IT'S OKAY TO NOT BE OKAY!

I made this heading bigger than usual because I am shouting (with love). Let's normalize getting help for our mental health. Reaching out to others in times of crisis is a sign of strength. Learning what made you vulnerable to a narcissist is just the beginning. I don't care what your mamma, great auntie or well meaning friend has told you, recovering from narcissistic relationships isn't a "you just need to get over it" kind of situation. Don't know where to start? I've also included the following resources.

RESOURCES

NATIONAL DOMESTIC VIOLENCE HOTLINE
For more information on narcissistic relationships and emotional abuse as well as intimate partner violence call, text or visit the following website:

(1.800.799.SAFE (7233) or text "START" to 88788)
https://www.thehotline.org/resources/narcissism-and-abuse/

POST TRAUMATIC STRESS DISORDER (PTSD)
PTSD is a psychological INJURY (read that again) caused by traumatic events. For more information on symptoms and treatment:

(NAMI Helpline at **800-950-NAMI (6264)** or chat is available. **In a crisis? text "NAMI" to 741741)**
https://www.nami.org/Blogs/NAMI-Blog/November-2017/PTSD-and-Trauma-Not-Just-for-Veterans

Suicide Hotline
Dial 988
The Lifeline provides 24/7, free and confidential support for people in distress, prevention and crisis resources. 988 has been designated as the new three-digit dialing code that will route callers to the National Suicide Prevention Lifeline.

(1-800-273-8255)
https://suicidepreventionlifeline.org/ **Chat** is available on the website.

Mental Health is Heath
Not sure what you're experiencing? This site will help you explore your feelings and includes links to 24/7 support.

https://www.mentalhealthishealth.us/

World Narcissistic Abuse Awareness Day (June 1st)
For more information do a Google deep dive for pages dedicated to education and support.

Notes: _____

_____

_____

_____

Notes:

Made in United States
North Haven, CT
30 September 2023

42201320R00057